Th...
GR...
in m...

Loss of a Parent

GRIEVERS LIBRARY

Take Comfort. Take a Book.

our mission

Grievers Library offers the companionship of books to those among us living with grief.

Borrow a book you need; return a book you no longer need.

learn more at:
www.grieverslibrary.org

Loss of a Parent

Adult Grief when Parents Die

Theresa Jackson

First published in August 2014
Reprinted in 2016 and 2017

Stay up to date with the latest books, special offers,
and exclusive content from Theresa Jackson by
signing up to our newsletter, or following her on
Goodreads.

Support Indie publishers.

DEDICATION

This book is dedicated to my late father, Simon, who never failed to pick me up when I fell, or come running when there was something wrong. I hope wherever he is now that he would be proud of me, as I was of him. One of my fondest memories of him is when he took me to my university halls of residence for the first time, and out of all the parents that were there, he was the only one laughing, joking, and being friendly to everyone. I've never been prouder. Here's to you, dad, your soft heart, and one of the best senses of humour I've ever known.

ACKNOWLEDGMENTS

I would like to thank my family for coming together at a time of immense grief and confusion for all of us. In particular my mother, who despite having been divorced from my father for over ten years at the time of his passing, helped her three children to get through the loss and subsequent life-turmoil. We were young adults, shoved into a house that mildly resembled a hoarders' time-capsule, pulled out of our lives, and having to make the best of it. Tensions ran high at times, but we muddled through in the end. Mum would arrive with bags of groceries or take us out for a meal to offer respite from the heavy task of clearing and renovating during the long weeks that followed.

PROLOGUE

This book is split into three sections, the first looking at how grief affects you, your emotions and your body, giving various sets of circumstances. I've included my own account of what I went through when I lost my father in 2007, my thoughts and feelings, and those of many others, to help you put your own experiences into context and see that you are not alone.

In this book I try to use my own experience, and that of others to give help to people who have recently (or not so recently) lost a parent. Bereavement is hard and if you've never experienced it before, it can be unexpectedly devastating and bewildering. For me it was as though I had stepped outside of my world, couldn't gain perspective, or see the way back in.

The second section looks at the effects on the family. It deals with the emotional aspects of funerals, inheritance, and even communication and conflict resolution skills, as some families can find that difficult times such as this lead to heightened sensitivity, the flare up of historical tensions and a great deal of upset and unrest whilst the family adapts to the new "normal."

The third section looks at recovery, and is mostly made of practical exercises. These can help you process your emotions healthily, keep memories alive, and improve your wellbeing and happiness. To make notes on a tablet, press and hold the screen and select the menu option to add notes. There is no "magic healing button," so these exercises won't heal your pain, but they might help you understand and process what you are feeling so that you can move forwards, slowly, and minimize the risk of a complicated or "stuck" pattern of grieving, where you feel as though you cannot come to terms with your loss.

CONTENTS

Introduction

First, may I start by saying I am so sorry that you find yourself reading this book. I would not usually start a book this way, but losing a parent is one of the most difficult parts of life, that most people go through at some point.

I, myself, lost my father at the end of 2007, from a heart attack, which is the reason I decided to write this book. Eighteen months earlier he had suffered a debilitating stroke that left him a virtual vegetable in a bed. Slowly and painstakingly he had fought for recovery and was immensely happy to be alive. He had reached the point of being able to live a mobile, happy life, only to be lost unexpectedly.

Although I cannot know your personal circumstances, or where your emotional journey will take you, I can start by saying sorry for your loss. I'm sorry that you find yourself in this most horrible of clubs that nobody ever wants to join. And I can reassure you that you are not alone in what you are going through.

Although there are various recognised states during grief, the process of grieving is different for everybody. This book will be looking at many different people's stories, to give you an idea that different reactions and grief pathways are to be expected, and no two people are the same when dealing with grief.

When a parent dies, the length of time taken to grieve, and the intensity and difficulty in coming to terms with their death can depend on many things. The relationship experienced with the parent, the way in which they died, and the personality and stage of life of the child can all be factors.

If your relationship with your parent was happy, if things were left unsaid, if there were conflicts, misunderstandings or abuse, the chance to resolve the problem in life is, sadly, gone. You are no longer directly affected by your parent- whether positively or negatively. Grief involves these realities being realised, and working out a way to find peace and resolution in mind and spirit.

In addition to this, a person who at one time in our lives appeared immortal and infallible has become mortal and vulnerable. As a result, we may feel loneliness and a sense of vulnerability ourselves. How can we feel secure in life if we have so little control over such important matters? This can be very difficult to deal with.

It is estimated that approximately 10% of people who experience grief for a parent will go on to develop complicated or prolonged grief, whereby they are unable to process the grief properly (which may have later repercussions) or become stuck in a state of grief and unable to progress back towards normal life.

In this case, professional counselling, support groups and practical exercises (such as those in the final section) can be very effective at helping to process grief. If in doubt, seek professional advice or call a free grief support service for advice (see the final section for website details of free services in the U.S.A. and U.K.).

For those who do not experience prolonged or complicated grief, the generally accepted phases of grief for an adult or child who has lost a parent are an initial sense of shock or denial, turbulent emotions and thoughts including anger, confusion, and deep sorrow, followed by depression and despair, as realisation of reality occurs. These states can pass at different rates, do not necessarily come in order, can move back and forth. Finally, the adult child eventually begins to come to terms with the loss whilst keeping a sense of relationship with the absent parent.

Many people find that how they feel following a loss, comes as a complete surprise. Unwanted thoughts, feelings and reactions can arrive, unbidden and disappear just as suddenly, giving the feeling of a complete loss of control over what you're experiencing.

It's important that when dealing with the loss of a parent you try and treat yourself kindly, or with "kiddy gloves." Far too often people neglect their own emotional needs trying to meet the demands of everyday life. Finding some time to yourself to process your grief can help immensely. Your perspective on life, mortality and human vulnerability can feel as though they have been radically changed. You won't get to fully understand your new perspective on life until after the grief has passed.

This kind, gentle attitude also goes for the rest of the family. It can be helpful to recognise that other people will deal with loss in their own way. Just as you may come to forgive yourself for any unwelcome thoughts, feelings or reactions, you might also try and forgive your family members for any strange behaviour which may not fit with your own personal view of how to grieve or behave.

Section 1

Grief and Emotions for your Lost Parent

1

In this section we'll examine some commonly experienced stages of grief, acknowledging that these stages may come and go, or never arrive, and that everyone has a unique experience.

The shock of an unexpected death may bring different thoughts and feelings when compared with a death following a long illness, which is the most common scenario when adult children lose a parent. It's not uncommon to experience mixed and confusing emotions, as we see from the experiences of others.

We'll look at stories of people coming to terms with their own mortality, after losing such a core part of who they are, and how bereavement can be complicated by difficult relationships, regrets and things left unsaid.

The Grief Cycle

It is often thought that grief occurs in predictable stages, with some people expecting that a person in mourning may flow from one stage to the next.

This is not the case, as grief is a highly personalised emotional journey, with steps forwards, backwards, containing a wide mix of emotions and stages. They can occur in any order or not at all, and as you will see from the range of stories you will read, they do not follow a timetable, or any rules that you might like them to follow.

Despite this, it can be useful to know what you might expect to experience on your journey. There are thought to be 5 to 7 common stages of bereavement, known as the Kubler-Ross model of loss, shown in the diagram.

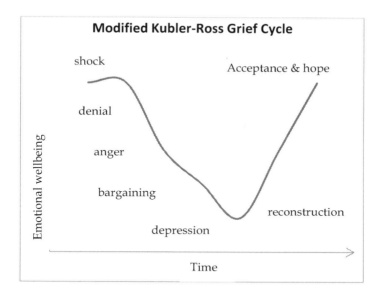

The seven stages of grief (modified from Kubler-Ross five stages of grief)

We won't go into large amounts of detail on each of these stages, as this book focuses more on the stories and experiences of others that might give you context for your own feelings, as well as practical exercises for you to do that might help you, rather than looking at the theoretical aspects of grief. But it is still good to know and have a basic idea of what the different stages might be.

Shock, denial and isolation: Immediately after death feelings of numbness and loneliness are common. In my case, activities carried on as normal for the first week, as if nothing had changed, and there was only a strange sense that something large had shifted underfoot. I spoke with my friends and colleagues as normal, and didn't tell most of them a thing about what had happened. In other cases, the initial shock can be an incredibly painful experience. We look more at initial reactions later in the "immediately after a death" section.

Anger, yearning and bargaining: You may feel an enormous sense of loss, and feel you would do anything to make it stop, put things right, or not face up to reality. I found this stage particularly confusing, as though a fog had descended on my brain, everybody had something I wanted (a dad) and it wasn't fair at all.

Details of life in the future, and how things will change start to occur to you, and for me these triggered feelings of rejection towards the change. Unfortunately, I had no control over the change and had to accept it anyway. Realization that there is nothing you can do led to the next stage for me, a terrible feeling of hopelessness and lack of control over life in general.

Depression and despair: The enormity of loss sinks down on you, the world is bleak, you realize nothing will be the same again. Life seems fragile and delicate and as though it could fall apart at any moment.

This stage may last longer than some people realize, as after time you can appear to function normally to the outside world, but on the inside, nothing seems to matter. For me, the triviality of social conversations became so overwhelming that I withdrew from most of my friends, and had to force myself to be "fun" when what I really felt like doing was having nothing to do with anyone.

Testing, hope, acceptance and reorganization: Eventually, so long as there are no complicated circumstances that prevent you from grieving, things start to get a little better. You find ways to get through your difficult feelings and solutions finally arrive.

A feeling of acceptance may then follow, and can

feel quite comforting. Guilt, anger and despair give way to positive memories and a feeling that you are at peace, although still emotional at times, with your loss.

2

Immediately After a Death

I don't remember getting the news that my father had died, it is blocked from my mind almost entirely. I think it may have been my mom who broke it to me, although they had been divorced for several years at the time. I do remember that I was at home, in my new apartment in South Korea where I was teaching English, and that all around me, my carefully constructed world stood still, waiting until I breathed out and let it crumble.

He had died whilst on holiday with his girlfriend, Gertrude, in Belgium. A heart attack, following a year and a half of slowly recovering from a devastating stroke that had left him entirely unable to move.
Slowly he had fought his way back from a state of infancy, not able to recognise anybody, to moving

an arm, a leg, sitting, wheeling around, and then finally the jubilant day when he could walk. His previous eloquence lost and replaced by a confusing fruit salad of words, but with his old charm still remaining. He may have seemed a sandwich short of a picnic, but he had enough of his wits about him to effortlessly charm the nurses into a dance or two with his disarmingly lovable mischief. He was only 53 when he died.

It felt as though a fundamental shift was taking place inside me. A parent that was present during my upbringing felt like such a fundamental part of my identity that it was as though "everything changed" quietly in an instant.

In the short time between his death and the funeral, all I felt was numbness and shock. Despite this I remember continuing on as though not much had changed, but I needed constant company, and when I was alone I would sleep continuously. Other people have said that they felt completely the opposite. They needed to be alone, or had a strange energy that stopped them relaxing or being able to do nothing.

The days following dad's death felt as though I were stuck in a strange kind of administrative limbo, where hymns, prayers and poems suddenly mattered. Casket wood, casket linings, choosing a photograph of remembrance, flowers, black shoes, black dresses. All suddenly important. All so meaningless. It was so surreal. I could not really start to move on to the process of grieving properly until after the funeral.

Depending on your circumstances, you may find that you need to return to regular daily life a lot faster than you feel able to cope with. The rest of the world carries on as normal, although nothing feels normal with you, and far too often there are few people around who make allowances for, or are even aware of your situation.

For me, I returned to work as normal the next day, and told no one. It was part of a coping mechanism that helped me pretend nothing had happened. The hardest part was when people found out my news, and suddenly I had no one to pretend with. Everyone was full of condolences, embarrassed or sad for me, and I felt like an alien being watched for the smallest of emotional cues.

Unfortunately, whilst I preferred no one to mention it for fear of breaking down, others can find this avoidance of the subject the most hurtful part of returning to the real world after a loss. It's difficult for others to know what to do, but a genuine heartfelt enquiry after how you are doing, even at the risk of upsetting you can mean a lot at such a difficult time.

Charlotte's Story
Charlotte sadly lost her mother to cancer at 1am on Christmas Eve, and recalled the unexpected pain that she felt. Unlike myself, she remembers all of the details exactly, and even sensed it before she was told. For her, she recalls such excruciating, unbearable pain that she found herself howling "like an animal" and felt like throwing herself under a car to be released from her suffering. The same day was spent dealing with formalities, like paperwork death certificates and funeral directors, all of which seemed completely inappropriate at a time when she was in such pain.

All around her people were doing their Christmas shopping as Charlotte sat in disbelief, with the same thought repeating and repeating in her head. Her mother had just died. She cried without shame in a café whilst waiting to collect the death certificate from the Town Hall.

She told everyone who would listen that her mother had just died from cancer, and heard stories back from a woman whose daughter had just died from cancer two months ago. She felt as though she had joined a club that she never wanted to be in. Charlotte's mind raced constantly with memories forming endless pictures in her mind.

Going into Shock

Experiencing a parent die, at any age, usually ends up with us going into a state of shock. This is a pattern, and we're not alone. A lot of our strange behaviour and feelings or thoughts are the same for many people. One of the main features of shock is that reactions to emotional trauma are different to how you might expect them to be.

You can see by comparing my reaction to losing my dad to Charlotte's reaction to losing her mum, that shock be an entirely different experience as well.

My reaction was numbness, where my mind only let me start to process my deeper emotions when I was safe, and Charlotte's reaction was full-force, brutally stinging, shocking pain.

Everyone's reaction immediately after a loss is different. Don't expect to react as you would like to, and don't apply these expectations to other people. Honour your journey, and trust that if you feel numb, your shock will get you through.

If you experienced a "numb" reaction like mine you may have felt able to return to work, you could have planned trips, activities, socialising, you may even feel that your reaction is entirely inappropriate to what has happened. Some people even feel a euphoric urgency to "get on with life" and busy themselves to the point of distraction.

You might also feel agitated and nervous, get bored of trivial conversations, zone out, or forget things. It is not unusual to have very vivid dreams in the immediate days after death, such as farewell dreams or dreams about death or dying. It is also common not to be able to sleep at all.

The first month will most likely be a foggy blur. You may have a lot of things to take care of, such as life insurance, credit cards, bills companies. All the while you may feel as though nothing has happened, or you're ready to rip somebody's head off, or roll over and give yourself up for dead. Thankfully, a lot of the details will get lost in this fog, and you probably won't remember them. This is your brain looking after you. There's no need to worry or feel bad about this fog. Even though it may feel all encompassing, it is not. And it will not last forever.

Delirium

Both myself and my grandparents went into an unexpected type of shock when my father was initially taken ill, and we thought we might lose him,
eighteen months before he passed. I don't wish to cause anybody any offence, or to appear cold, but we found the most inappropriate of things, very, very funny. And when I say funny, I mean hysterical to the point of delirium.

I still recall the three of us waiting in the hospital intensive care unit "family meeting room" with my grandparents for a doctor. We were going to discuss whether we might expect my father to survive, and if so to what extent he might recover from his vegetative state.

We were embarrassed because we couldn't stop laughing. We were laughing about infidelity, divorce, affairs, money, life, death. All of which were incredibly inappropriate subjects to laugh about. And yet we couldn't stop. Thankfully when the doctor arrived we came down to earth, or rather sank into our respective pits of depression and worry, as they simply couldn't tell us what would happen.

Something similar had happened to me on my way over to the hospital, on the plane from Australia where I had been traveling. The airline had made an extra effort to get me on board a last-minute flight, because of the urgent circumstances, and the cabin crew were being wonderfully kind to me.

As we took off I lost myself in several episodes of comedy on my personal video screen, and found myself laughing loudly for most of the flight. By the time we landed the same crew were giving me some very sceptical looks, which probably should have shamed or embarrassed me. But I only found it funny. I simply didn't care about these very kind peoples' opinions.

This baffles me to this day, as I am quite a sensitive and thoughtful person on the most part. It simply makes me marvel at the capability of our brains to send us into shock, delirium, or whatever we need to see us through and protect us until we are safe to process incredibly difficult emotions.

The only thing that I can think of, is that laughter has always been one of my coping mechanisms. I use it to feel better about all kinds of things, and to self-soothe.

Once, in a drama class when I was thirteen, we had a physical instructor "drill" us by shouting in our faces and making us do press ups. I couldn't help but giggle uncontrollably, and when he came along to shout in my face, I promptly burst into tears, which brought the whole exercise to an end. In my case, I guess, the saying you either laugh or cry are especially apt.

Try not to be too hard on someone who goes a little "delirious" even if this is not how you would react and find it offensive or shocking. Their brain may not be ready to face the truth yet. However, you and your family react to the shock, try and just let it wash over you and let it be.

3

The End of a Life-Long Relationship

The death of a parent marks the end of your active relationship with them, and a point at which nothing can be changed. For me, every memory had to be worked through and sorted and "tagged" with an update: he was no longer with me, so that when memories visited me, I would remember him in a way that felt forever changed. I felt tired and slept a lot, as though my mind was doing a great deal of secret "behind the scenes" work.

It may be surprising to know, that whilst it can feel as though your relationship has ended it has not. I'm not talking religion, I'm talking about an inner sense of carrying your parent with you, in memories and in spirit wherever you are, which is exactly how I and many others feel.

My memories of my father will remain with me always, but I also call on him for strength and guidance from time to time, and feel as though he is still there. It can take a long time to readjust to this "distant" relationship, but for me it is this new, continuing relationship that allows me to hold onto the memories of him happily.

In a lot of cases memories of a parent may be difficult to recall, in the first year or two of bereavement, but try not to worry or feel guilty about this- they come back with time. You are not a bad son or daughter, and nor are you betraying or forgetting them, if you cannot remember much at this time, your brain may be blocking out some of your memories at present.

My brother once told me that he couldn't remember dad at all, and my sister the same thing. Both told me this within the first few months of him passing, and I have to say that it was difficult to remember who he was and what he looked like as well. Not being able to remember does not say a thing about how much you loved them, it says that your brain is in a state of confusion, flux or change.

One of the underlying shifts following my father's death was getting used to the fact that I was no longer protected by him. Parents look after us during our childhood, and many continue to do so in adulthood. When this feeling of protection is taken away, it can result in an intense feeling of vulnerability and loneliness.

The unconditional love that there once was, is no longer there to provide support. This varies from one person to the next, and can depend upon the relative ages of the bereaved and the parent, as well as the nature of the relationship and personalities involved. If both parents are now lost or absent the feeling of being alone in the world can be very frightening.

Elina's story

Elina's father died of an unexpected heart attack in 1999, and it was her first experience of bereavement, which was so shocking she describes it as like a "punch to the stomach." Five years on her mother also died and at the age of forty she felt like an orphan, anchorless and drifting, like the "only tree left standing in a forest."

She felt as though they were the one constant and stable point across her whole life, despite being a fully-fledged adult who could stand on her own and support herself. Years after their deaths she still finds herself biting her tongue when her friends complain of having to visit their parents during the holidays, reminding them that they should enjoy them while they can, before an uncomfortable silence and subject change.

She finds other people get very uncomfortable if she brings up the fact that she has no parents, to a point where it's almost embarrassing. The awkwardness is frustrating and stupid to her mind, and she believes that most of us are more the same than different, with these different life events and stages bonding us. Experiencing the bereavement of your parents is something almost everyone will go through at some point in their lives.

Elina now feels completely comfortable with her memories, and enjoys thinking about the happy times that she shared with her parents. She misses them, but draws on her memories as a source of strength when she is going through life's challenges and feels alone. That way she is still able to feel lucky to have been brought up by two loving parents.

4

Thoughts and Emotions

Whilst struggling to come to terms with loss, many people will experience a tidal wave of thoughts and emotions that may churn and reoccur constantly or appear so suddenly and unexpectedly that it is surprising. Many people wonder if their thoughts are normal. Disbelief or denial of what has happened may occur and remain for many months or even years, along with confusion and worry.

It may feel to the bereaved as though they are going mad, with no rhyme or reason for their troubled thought patterns. These thoughts can occur at any time of day or night and do not respect schedules. Disrupted sleep and nightmares are common, which can exacerbate disrupted thought patterns and confusion.

Guilt

Some people may blame themselves for the loss, thinking that there may have been something that they could have done to save their parent. If only they'd tried harder, called more often, or done more.

As I mentioned earlier, I was living in South Korea when my father died, and I hadn't seen him for the year before he passed. When I had left he was recovering well from his stroke. I had been traveling in Australia when he had had his stroke and I had come home immediately and spent six months with him, visiting him in hospital until the glorious release back to his home and freedom, and then two further months feeling such pride for him in his recovery. I treasure those memories so deeply. He was so happy to be alive, and so determined to get himself better. Perhaps a little optimistically he dreamed of getting back on his motorbike one day.

However, I felt terribly guilty that I hadn't seen him before he died, and had looked forward to returning to him so much. Our long-distance chess games meant so much to him and me, as did the calls from afar, but guilt still lingered on.

Despite not being able to string a coherent sentence together, and using all kinds of "word substitutes" (such as "kitchen sink" to mean "everything," borrowed from the phrase "I've packed everything except the kitchen sink") and taking about 20 attempts to dial a phone number, he beat me at every long-distance chess game we played. He even told me how to ski when I was giving it my first and only attempt (if in doubt throw yourself on the floor before you get too fast, and if you're going too fast, just lean to one side and ski uphill. Brilliant, thanks dad).

The guilt lingered despite being urged to go and follow my long-standing dreams of working abroad by everyone in the family, including him. The situation at home had unfortunately turned ugly as my father's girlfriend held unusually strong hostilities towards his children. I don't hold this against her as she had suffered a large amount of psychological turmoil culminating in a nervous breakdown shortly before they had met a few years earlier.

His stroke had set her all the way back to square

one, and she wanted them to be left alone, and guarded him ferociously. He never let it reach him-he was wonderful about it, and never let her drive his children away, to the best of his ability. His outlook remained positively and inspiringly sunny. In fact, I remember how proud he was (and we all were) when after six months recovery he was able to do a one-armed press up with his strong arm.

Despite being reassured that "you can't not live your life because of what ifs" and that I should get out into the world and make my "dreams happen," when he died before I got home, not seeing him again seemed totally unacceptable. I agree with all the advice that I was given. You can't live your life based on "what ifs," and he seemed to be completely on the mend when I had left. But from an instinctive gut-level, it felt like I should have been there, no matter what I was putting on hold, or what hostility I faced.

This kind of guilt and sadness are common, particularly if there is something you feel you could have done or said differently, or if you feel as though your parent may not have known how you felt about them. People may go around in circles punishing themselves until these feelings run their course. If this is the case for you, try and realise that guilt is a part of bereavement, and that most people will feel guilty about something, and pick on themselves about not having done something differently.

Try and focus instead on the fact that most people feel this guilt. Your parent would not want you to feel this way. They probably knew that you loved them, and in real life, people don't walk around acting as though they are afraid that every action, conversation or interaction might be the last one. It is not a healthy way to live.

It really is quite likely that the last conversation or meeting you have with someone before they die, will be ordinary, perhaps snippy, perhaps annoyed, or perhaps you were lucky enough that it was nice or loving. But this is just a reflection of real life.
It isn't realistic to expect to be perfectly loving and ready for death all the time, just in case somebody dies. And in the case of long term illnesses, it isn't realistic or what your parent would want, for your life to have been put on hold because you are "waiting" for them to die.

Krista's Story
Krista was a young adult when she lost her mother to bowel cancer. She recalls how the final week of her mother's life was spent arguing because her mother wanted her to go home and live with her instead of the man that she thought she loved (and later found out to be wrong).

She regrets that her final words with her mum were angry, and that she didn't tell her she loved her and thought she was an incredible inspiration. After years of guilt she eventually came to terms with the fact that even though their last words were angry, her mum knew that she loved her, and that it was this that was important rather than one single moment or one single week.

Seven years on, she still misses her and having someone to fall on in times of hardship. But she describes her mom as an inspiration and a supporter.

Lisa's Story
Lisa suffered immense guilt because she and her family presumed that her mother's pains and

symptoms of an undiscovered multiple myeloma were part of her type two diabetes. She felt as though she didn't take her mum's pains or complaints seriously, and wishes she had listened to her, blaming herself for not getting medical care sooner.

Three months were lost in getting her treatment because of this, and because of consulting with the "wrong doctors" about it, who she felt were "irresponsible" and negligent.

After some time, she came to realise that despite the delay there would have been no cure, and that her guilt was part of her grief. She was not to know that her mother's pains were different from any of the others, and she could not have known what this meant if she did. Even though she knows this, she still berates herself for not sparing her mother more of her pain with a better palliative care program.

Anger and Blame

In contrast to guilt, feelings of anger and blame towards a parent may emerge, "how could they leave me alone" and "how could they do this to me" are typical thoughts and can create shame. You may feel that to have these thoughts you must be a bad person. These feelings are typical, particularly because parents protected us and guided us into the world.

Katherine's Story

Katherine's grew up with an alcoholic father, and an emotionally unavailable mother, who tried to kill herself several times. Her parents divorced when she was thirteen, and she started drinking herself during her teenage years, but stopped when she met her partner who didn't drink.

When she was in her thirties her dad passed away from liver failure, and she blamed him for not only his own death, but for her difficult start in life. At this time, she was hit by an unrelenting tidal wave of emotion- anger, blame, sadness- which she found incredibly difficult to get through.

A few years on, and Kathryn has spent a lot of time reflecting on her childhood, realising how her emotional needs had not been met as a child and how she had been so utterly unprepared to cope with the emotional challenge of losing her father. She realised that despite her circumstances, she was responsible for her emotions moving forward. She feels now that despite her incredibly difficult start in life, she's grateful for the lessons that she's learnt about herself, other people and life in general. She doesn't blame her father anymore, but misses him sometimes, hoping that he had the chance to reflect on his life before he passed away.

Relief
If a parent was ill prior to death, or even if you had a difficult relationship with them, it may result in the confusing and disturbing emotion of relief. Perhaps the bereaved is relieved that their parent is no longer suffering, or perhaps that their own suffering and waiting is over. It can be very stressful and upsetting when a parent is unwell, particularly if you are caring for them and you have deep wounds dating back to your childhood. Thoughts of relief may come, uninvited to mind, followed by feelings of guilt that such thoughts are evil or that you are a terrible person and ungrateful.

Every aspect of the change that loss has brought with it will need to be processed by the mind, and if there are objectively positive changes, then these will need to be acknowledged and processed too. This does not detract from the loving aspects of your relationship, and it does not mean that you have betrayed them. You can read more on these feelings later under "Death after Caregiving or Long Illness" and "Regrets and Difficult Relationships."

Confusion
There can be a great deal of confusion when a parent dies, over a whole host of issues. For example, you may feel as though you no longer have the same connection with your roots, and are lacking support. Other family members may start to remember your parent differently. Confusion over who gets to keep which keepsakes or what to do with inheritance can also be incredibly difficult, which I discuss later in the book.

Seeing Your Parent or Feeling Their Presence
In the year following dad's death I seemed to see him everywhere, but always out of the corner of my eye. Two years on and I spent some time awkwardly standing right next to a cardboard cut-out of a slightly younger version of my dad, and it gave me a profound sense of calm. I'm not sure if he noticed me creepily staring at him, but I couldn't seem to pull myself away.

It is common to see the deceased parent in different places, or see their likeness in the faces of others. Many people may still feel the presence of their parent, which can be comforting or unnerving.

5

Death after Caregiving or Illness

A typical death usually follows a long period of illness in which at least one member of the family gives care to their relative. If your parent was ill for a long period of time before they died, this can be very draining and exhausting on you and any others that looked after, cared for or worried about them. Illnesses are inherently unpredictable with a great deal of uncertainty and often suffering.

About one in five caregivers suffering from bereavement will have mental health issue, like depression or complicated grief (which is characterized by prolonged anguish and impairment of life in various aspects).

Recent research has shown that family members who are involved in providing care before death show much greater resilience and ability to adapt afterwards, with grief and depression symptoms returning almost to normal levels within a year. This is thought to be because they have had time to prepare for the impending death, have an absence of guilt over the caregiving they provided, and are relieved by the fact that their parent is no longer suffering or in need.

Grief following a period of illness can create some confusing thoughts and emotions, depending on the circumstances, because there is already usually a great deal of upset already, leading up to their passing. It has been found that the greater the level of distress before death, the more likely the chance of depression, anxiety or complicated grief afterwards. If you were highly burdened by caring for your parent, felt exhausted or overloaded with other responsibilities like work or caring for your own children then you are also more at risk of depression or complicated grief. It is important that you work through your grief and look after yourself properly.

We'll look at some stories from adult children who lost parents in different scenarios; such as those that were on the road to recovery (like my dad), those that were fighting a possibly curable disease (in this case cancer), and those that had a terminal illness (we look at Dementia).

Death When on the Path to Recovery

We were all very proud of my dad and his recovery. Eighteen months before he died he had suffered an enormous stroke and had been kept sedated for weeks on life support in an intensive care unit, miles away from his home. We didn't know if he would wake up at all, as each time the medical team tried to reduce his sedation, he would react badly and not be able to breath for himself. They couldn't tell us when (if) he woke up whether he would be a person, or a shell of his former self. All we could do was wait, and imagine him living a terrible life he'd never wanted, at the age of 51.

I had flown back from Australia where I'd been traveling the East coast in a van, my brother flew in from Korea where he was teaching English, and my little sister came straight from her school exams, which she had to take after hearing the news. How she managed to get through them I'll never know. Looking back, the entire experience was surreal.

The family congregated in Manchester and bunked like nursing students in onsite residential halls. Myself and my grandparents went into shock, reacting to the overwhelmingly scary situation by having deep, honest conversations about marriage and life. We probably overshared a little.

Watching a loved one slowly deteriorate, perhaps suffering hugely means that the family have been dealing with their own pain, as well as that of the dying parent. This can lead to feelings of helplessness that there is nothing that can be done to regain control, especially when the dying person no longer recognised their own children or spouse at the end of their life.

At the end, the fear of the inevitable loss is finally finished, and the grieving can begin. This can be really confusing, because with the death also brings an end to the pain of watching your loved one suffer. In this way, death can bring feelings of relief that the illness is finally over. This can be a terrible way to feel and although it is not uncommon, it may cause great shame and guilt and thoughts of being a terrible, unloving and selfish person.

Sometimes, over the course of long illnesses, grief can be experienced in advance of the actual death, and any unfinished business can be expressed, along with goodbyes. In this way, the shock of loss is lowered, and the family can be more prepared for life without their loved one. Funerals can be arranged in advance, and financial and pragmatic affairs can be settled. This can help significantly when it becomes time to grieve, however shock may still be experienced, and despite all preparations being made, emotions can still be more intense than expected.

Death after Fighting a Potentially Curable Illness

Sarah's Story

Sarah lost both of her parents to lung cancer before she or her sister had a chance to have children of their own. She and her sister cared for their dad in 2010 and saw how he fought so hard for the life that he loved so much. They were heartbroken as he lost his mobility and independence, and felt as though they were losing their foundations. They knew after he died that losing mother would be a nightmare.

Several years later, having rebuilt her life and set new paths, she got a call that her mother had stage

3 lung cancer. The family battled their way through two rounds of chemotherapy, but tragically, after nine months, there was recurrence in the bones, liver and brain. There were no surgical or chemotherapy options available, and after three more months her mother passed away. Sarah struggled with the fact that they had exhausted all treatment options, and that there was nothing more that could be done, but to let her mum go.

For weeks she felt nothing, her brain was protecting her with shock. She felt terrible about this, asking everyone why she wasn't upset or grieving. A counsellor told her that she had to wait, and that the numbness would subside to waves of paralysing pain. Soon enough crippling anguish engulfed her, and she could think of nothing but her mother and the cancer from morning until night.

She ached to hold her hand, and desperately wanted to speak to her. She wore her mother's clothes, sent her messages and emails, and even used her hairbrush. Sarah felt as though whoever she had been, ceased with her mother's death, and had left with her. Along with the unconditional love of a parent.

It was only when Sarah spoke to a friend who had lost her own parents recently that she started to take better care of herself. Tend to her own needs, as her friend told her she must. By forcing herself to eat well sleep for a full eight hours, and do regular exercise, Sarah felt better able to cope when she was hit by a wall of sadness. She regrets that her parents will never be grandparents, but she feels proud that she was able to give them love and care before they died. She's grateful that she had such good role models to teach her empathy, and hopes that she can do them proud by living her life in a caring way.

Death After a Terminal Illness

Steve's Story

Steve's father passed away five years ago, having battled with dementia for nine years. His mother was the primary caregiver, but Steve and his sisters helped whenever they could, as all the children lived in the neighbouring town.

Over the course of his father's illness, he spent his time learning all he could about the family stories. He learnt about how his mother and father met, and poured over every detail of their "courting" letters to one another. He talked to his mother about the stories behind each of the family photographs. In a way, he became the unofficial family historian. He and his sisters shared memories of their father and their childhood regularly, and enjoyed the first few years when their father could join in.

As he watched his father lose more and more of his memories each day, it was the stories that reminded him of what was true and right, and what mattered. The stories taught him that the important things to him were family, presence and love.

For him, he realised that whilst dementia was taking its toll on his father and their family, and even at the point of death, his family was being moulded and their story was still being written. He felt glad that he had contributed so much to his father's care over the years before he passed away.

6

Sudden, Unexpected Death

Everyone becomes bereaved at some point during their lifetimes. However, it is usually expected that this will follow illness or some form of warning that helps to prepare for the loss. When the loss of a parent is sudden and unexpected, or even if the parent has been ill and dying for some time, it can come as a shock and result in a great deal of overwhelming emotions.

Sudden grief can be traumatic, scary and devastating. Often people describe feelings of helplessness. The experience can feel dream-like and thoughts can become fragmented and confused as they struggle with the devastation.

The physical manifestations associated with sudden death can be related to trauma or stress reactions.

You might feel highly strung, nervous, jumpy or overly alert. Pacing around the house, forgetfulness such as forgetting why one entered a room, intrusive images or flashbacks.

As we age we learn that the journey of life can be shocking, but unfortunately although this lesson can help us somewhat, nothing can prepare for the sudden shock of death. The younger we are, the less we have come to realize that life is full of loss, and so young people may find themselves particularly unprepared to deal with such devastating circumstances.

Jen's Story

Jen was a critical care nurse when her mother died in a car accident, and found that she had to give up her profession as she could no longer cope with the stress or the trauma. She wasn't told about her mum's accident but simply found out that she had been admitted to the hospital where she worked.
She tragically witnessed her own mum die in front of her as part of her medical team, with no warning. The shock was intense, and she immediately fell to pieces, unable to work and sinking into a deep

depression.

She describes her mum as the person who believed that she was really great. She felt as though when her mother died, she took half of her away as well. It took Jen three years before she hit rock bottom, and started to piece her life back together. During that time, she completely withdrew from friends and isolated herself, spending most of her time alone. Recovery for Jen meant redirecting her life and her ambitions, putting new aspirations in place and reaching back out to old friends. She started to focus on building new relationships whilst strengthening old ones.

She also changed career, as she found the idea of returning to nursing too much for her to cope with. Working now as a dog walker, trainer and breeder, she spends her time outside in the sunshine, mostly with man's best friend.

She is much happier than she was, but still misses her mother and thinks of her most days. With her new life she enjoys the freedom to manage her own time, and does not miss her old hectic schedule from her nursing days.

She is considering becoming a part time nurse for individual patients, as getting to know people was always her favourite part of her nursing work and this way she could build long lasting relationships whilst still helping others. She didn't have much chance to build relationships as a critical care nurse as most of the patients were only in her care for a short while. That said she would never give up her dogs, and has her hands full now running training classes and looking after her pug bitch Molly, who is pregnant again for the second time.

Jen has come to realise that life doesn't always go to plan, but the important thing is to know when it is time to make a change, and start a new chapter in your life. She still carries the lessons that her mother taught her with her on the journey.

7

Grief in Young Adults

Young adults and teens are emerging from the process of forming their own identities, and if a parent dies during this time, it may have an impact on them for the rest of their lives. This does not mean that they will necessarily experience the pain indefinitely, but there may be consequences that arise from the loss.

For example, one young person may not be emotionally equipped to deal with the loss and may detach emotionally, only for grief to revisit them in convoluted ways during later life. Another young person may develop a positive character trait, such as a greater sense of responsibility.

Young people are by definition, in the process of forming their identities. Turbulent relationships that became difficult during adolescence may not be resolved until much later in life, if at all, and if this is thrown into the mix, the sense of grief and confusion can be multiplied several times over.

Young people and young adults tend to have or strive for strong peer groups. The death of a parent instantly makes them different from their friends. At my time of bereavement, I was 23, and this made me different from most of my friends, who were still able to call on their parents to dig them out of scrapes, pick them up and more importantly offer unconditional love and support.

Whilst my friends were having the times of their lives, I quickly fell from grace, became withdrawn, and found socialising significantly more difficult than I had previously. If I am honest, the effects of this can still be felt to this day, nine years later- I never fully regained my enthusiasm for socialising- it all just seemed too insignificant and petty, and I developed some degree of social anxiety.

In the case of my sister, who was 16 at the time that my father became ill and 18 at the time of his death, this was particularly difficult. My father had been at risk of a cardiovascular event for years prior to his stroke, all through my sister's teenage rebellious stage. The year before the stroke he had specifically told her that if he dropped dead from a heart attack or stroke, that it would be her fault due to the stress she had caused him. Now, don't get my father wrong, he was not a bad or evil man, he was simply human, very sensitive, and she was having troubles. However, the fact remains that his age, high body mass index, alcohol intake and smoking were the key risk factors associated with stroke. Laying guilt at my sister's feet was neither morally nor factually correct.

8

Regrets and Difficult Relationships

Parenting styles (generalised into four broad buckets on the following page) come with various difficulties for children, that don't necessarily correct themselves when they reach adulthood. Authoritarian, permissive and neglectful parenting styles often create difficulties in relationships between parents and children to one degree or another.

Sometimes, the death of a parent with whom you had a difficult relationship can bring these issues to the fore, making it very difficult to come to terms with the loss due to confusion, guilt, and things left unsaid.

Many people don't have the perfect relationship with their parents. Turbulent arguments, emotional, physical or sexual abuse, or just different personalities can lead to mixed or negative feelings between adult children and their parents. When dealing with the loss of a parent, memories from across the entire span of the relationship must be processed. These memories can be extremely painful and can make it much harder to move forward in the grieving process.

	High expectations for self-control	Low expectations for self-control
High sensitivity	Authoritative: Respectful of child's opinions, but maintains clear boundaries	Permissive: Indulgent, without discipline
Low sensitivity	Authoritarian: Strict disciplinarian	Neglectful: Emotionally uninvolved and does not set rules

Parenting styles and the corresponding effects on children

People that feel as though they had unfinished business with a parent can find it particularly hard to deal with the fact that they will not be able to finish it now. Perhaps feelings of love, hurt, anger or forgiveness were left unexpressed, and must now go unspoken. Negative feelings or memories of turbulent relationships mixed with feelings of love and loss may result in a confusing mix of sadness, anger towards one's parent or oneself, or shame.

My father and I experienced a "bad patch" during my teenage years, which thankfully had been discussed and resolved three or four years before he passed away. Still, memories of harsh words haunt me to this day, years after his death. This is the case even though I know we had moved on and shared some incredibly beautiful moments during those years.

Guilt and regret are common, as is denial or ambivalence. In some cases, denial is prolonged, as grieving is too difficult and cannot be faced. In these cases, grief can be buried and locked away, and may or may not return later.

For those who grieve but find it difficult to make sense of their mixed emotions, prolonged mourning may be a risk. Once somebody dies, especially a parent or close relationship, it becomes far more difficult to think or speak ill of them, which makes it hard to come to terms with the difficult thoughts that may arise.

Jan's Story
Jan found out that her mother was dead by text message, at the age of 26. She finished her shift as a waitress, before meeting her husband out, as she couldn't face going home. She hadn't spoken to her mum in two years, but prior to that they had been having regular calls. An argument resulted in her mother calling her an idiot, and it rang true against all the other times she'd been called worthless, a wimp, a coward, a little bitch, a whiner or useless. It was a tiny, insignificant breath, but it was the last breath of their relationship. When Jan hung up the phone, she wondered what to do. Her mother had been trying to be less cruel and abusive. She still wanted her to mother her, but she realised it was hopeless. She couldn't.

She suffered denial of her abuse at the hands of toxic friends and family who recognised that her mother had been motivated by the right things, but that weren't witness to the daily details of the verbal abuse that seemed so out of the realms of possibility to them. It took years but eventually Jan realised that in her death she was able to embrace her mother's love for her, and her love for her mother, but that the toxicity into which her mother had been born had sadly tainted their relationship to an incredibly painful degree.

She went on to find a positive, supportive community who provided her with the mothering she had so desperately wanted. She remembers how warm her mother could be, and recognises that she had good intentions most of the time, that were sadly ruined by her lack of self-control.

Section 2:

Grief in the Family

9

When a parent dies, it is likely that an entire family will go into mourning. It can be very difficult to see the people that you care about in pain. If both parents were together at the time of death, watching the remaining parent struggle to cope can be tragic for the entire family. However, if your parents were divorced, you may struggle with feelings that the deceased parent, their way of life, and a good part of your childhood has been lost and forgotten about.

Adult children and remaining spouses must find a new equilibrium and way of living together and supporting each other. Roles within the family must be adjusted to make up for the loss, and this can take time. Often people find that the entire family dynamic changes, and this must be accepted and become normal and habitual before life can continue peacefully.

Changes to your Family

When there is a death in a family, there is a new void in the family system. The family will have to adjust around this change to find a new balance. This adjustment will be created by those who remain, and how it happens will depend on each member of the family's age, role, attitude towards bereavement, and the stage of grief they are experiencing.

Each family member must go through the process of realising that they have changed because of the loss, and then put this change into practice in their life. A family can either help or hinder this process.

Anniversaries

Times of anniversaries may be particularly difficult for the family system to adjust to, such as the anniversary of the day your parent died, birthdays and holidays. These days can help by being a set time where a family has "permission" to grieve. Rituals like going to a grave or holding a religious service can help in the sharing. However, this isn't always a good thing, as feelings of grief can be compounded into long-term unresolved grief.

If you want to commemorate your parent, but in a healthy way, you might find that doing one of the activities in Section 3 allows you to strike this balance between poignancy and meaning, and compounding unresolved grief.

Toby's Story

For the first three years after Toby's father passes away, his family gathered together on his dad's birthday and shared stories. His sister brought his dad's favourite chips- Doritos- and his mother plays "their song." They shared a glass of wine together and tried to make the remembrance a celebration of his father's life, talking about his best moments in life. He felt that this helped to keep his memory and legacy alive. After three years the family decided to grieve in their own ways, but they still talk about his dad in conversation regularly.

Linda's Story

Linda's mother died on her birthday five years ago. Since then she has found it difficult to celebrate her birthday, seeing it only as a day of sadness and grief. Her family spend little time or attention on her as they are all focusing on remembering her mother. Next year, she has decided that she will celebrate her birthday, and the life of her mother by going to a restaurant with her husband. She knows that her mother would want her to take this more positive approach.

Family Emotional Reactions

A common reaction to anger and guilt is to displace your feelings, to defend against feeling them directly. This needs a scapegoat, which might be inside the family or outside (like doctors and medical services). This scapegoat figure can keep a family together as someone or something to blame, projecting anger onto them. Guilt can also be redirected into a need to punish yourself or others, feeling as though you deserve it. Paranoia, shame and embarrassment are also common.

Overprotective behaviour might rear its head, for fear of a similar fate visiting a remaining family member. This can lead to increased guardedness against outsiders, individuals being unable to grieve alone and a lack of privacy or space. An increased dependency on remaining family after the loss of a parent is natural, but it can be unhealthy and lead to a family being isolated from their community, with only each other for solace.

There is sometimes a difference between how different generations in the same family deal with grief. In situations where both parents were still in partnership at the time of death, it is not only their own grief that an adult child must cope with, but also the pain of the other parent. This can be extremely sad and difficult to deal with, and may lead to prolonged stress and unhappiness within a family. Many people who are widowed find the second year of grieving even more difficult than the first.

Members of families with parents who were separated or divorced at the time of death, or a family that is dysfunctional in some other way, can find it confusing when a parent passes away. If the remaining parent has moved on to a new life, it can feel as though the lost parent has been forgotten.

When someone dies, they may become an idealized version of themselves. Some people will be unable to let go of an image of them as perfect, placing them on a pedestal. This can be a dangerous road to take, as if it is take to extremes, it can prevent the living from moving on and bonding with the living, or creating new relationships. It can result in a tendency to live in the past, with an individual's identity frozen in time and attached to the dead parent. This can manifest with someone trying to keep everything the same as it was when the parent was alive.

In some cases, a family member may try and replace the lost loved one with somebody else, before the grieving process has run its course. My friend, Dave, lost his father to lung cancer, and his devastated mother busied herself frantically, not stopping for a second. Dave found his family at loggerheads when his mother revealed that a year after his father's death his mother had started a relationship with his uncle, reaching out to each other in their grief. Eventually Dave reconciled himself with the knowledge that he had no choice but to accept the new relationship, which his brothers also had to accept to keep the family together.

Most families will go under a degree of restructuring, with siblings taking on parental roles and relationships strengthening across the generations. In some cases, marriages can be damaged because of these changes in role, and can even lead to divorce.

10

Funerals, Inheritance and Getting Along

Funerals can be difficult both to arrange and attend, for functioning or dysfunctional families alike. It may well be that death brings out the best in family members who try and help and support others to pick up the pieces. However, it is just as common for these difficult times to bring out the worst in strained relationships.

The funeral itself holds different representations to different people, some may see it as a religious ceremony, others a way of saying goodbye or gaining some form of closure, a way of showing respect, or a celebration. All viewpoints are different, and can result in different needs and wants amongst the living.

Deciding what to do and who performs what role

can be easy, or surprisingly difficult. Hopefully, everyone is easy going and moves forwards together to ensure that the funeral is an experience that everyone is happy with. In my case the funeral was easily arranged. Granny had some wishes that were important to her, dad's girlfriend, Gertrude, had some wishes that were important to her, and his children and my grandfather were simply sad, despondent and had nothing we felt we needed. To us, nothing would bring him back and it all seemed futile. To granny and Gertrude, they wanted to say goodbye in a poignant and beautiful way. Thankfully, nobody's requests overlapped each other which made things simple.

Occasionally, deep feelings of hurt or resentment can arise, and are exacerbated by the troubled emotions of grief. People may not approach funerals with a clear mind, and this is good to know. It means that in situations where disagreements arise, if nothing else can be taken away, it can at least be understood that the conflict has arisen due to intense emotions, a difficult situation, and a lack of clarity of thought on both sides.

The Will, Estate and Inheritance

For those that need to, executing a will, sorting through your parent's possessions, estate and bills can be extremely stressful. Where sentimental keepsakes become involved dealing with "who gets what" is an area following death that can go perfectly smoothly, but also holds the potential to cause enormous family rifts and resentments. In the best-case scenario everyone is happy with their role in administering the estate, are happy with who would like to keep different mementos, how the estate is to be split, and the final words within the will.

Sadly though- on occasion- people can walk away feeling begrudged, and if this is not addressed it may cause a family rift that can take years to heal or never be healed. If possible, it is best to turn the other cheek during difficult times, and attempt to be easy going- it may save a lot of heart ache in future.

Children who inherit money from their parent, no matter how large or small, may experience a great deal of pressure over what to do with it. Some may feel that they don't need it, want it or deserve it, whilst others have no trouble in accepting that their parent intended for them to inherit what they receive and feel free to put it to whatever purpose they choose.

I've spoken to some people who felt compelled to plan how to make use of their inheritance and then felt guilty about doing so, as though they were betraying their parent. Inheritance also can come with an emotional price tag. It is usually money that has been worked very hard for by your parent, built up slowly over time and even with the exact intention that it becomes your inheritance. Feelings of pressure that the money must be "used well" or carefully spent in a way that the parent would agree with can weigh heavily on the mind of the bereaved, and stop your life from flowing in the direction that you would want it to.

David's Story
David struggled for years with feeling that he did nothing to deserve the large inheritance that he received, never got the chance to prove himself or "make it" by himself, and have felt a bizarre sense of responsibility that he must somehow use it to do something "extraordinary," instead of having just an ordinary, normal life (which is what he would have liked).

Eventually he decided to buy a home and start his own business, after which David realised that he could spend much of the rest of his inheritance on making his life more comfortable from day to day. He put a portion of the money into his pension fund, bought a rental property, and slowly spent the remainder on annual holidays for his family.

11

Conflict Over the Will

According to recent research by a leading will-writing service, there are clear warning signs that there will be a conflict over inheritance. Losing a family member is excruciating enough, without the turmoil and pain of family infighting. If that wasn't reason enough to try and work things out amicably, nine times out of ten those who go to war over inheritance end up worse off overall, with the only guaranteed winner being the lawyer.

So, what are the top red flags that something could go wrong in your family? The first is sibling rivalry, where the settlement of an estate can at times become more about settling old scores than about doing what the deceased would have wanted. This is confounded if there is a disparity between how wealthy the heirs are. A difference in wealth can lead to differences in decisions, such as whether to sell straight away or hold onto an asset.

If there are multiple executors to an estate, estranged children, disinherited family members, late marriages or if one heir receives an advanced benefit compared to others, this can result in differences in opinion and conflict is more likely as a result. In the next section, we'll look at conflict resolution techniques, but hopefully with a little understanding, these won't be necessary.

James' Story
James grew up with an older sister, Liz, and a younger brother, Neil, in a household where money was rather tight. He emphasised the fairness of his early upbringing, with everyone getting the same number of presents at Christmas, and the same amount of pocket money. He insists that they were a very normal family. Normal, until years later the family ended up in court over a devastating family rift.

Liz was a writer, with not much by way of a fortune, and had been the main caregiver to their dying mother for eighteen months before she died. James on the other hand was a successful, self-made business man- pride of the family- with a multi-million-dollar bank balance. This was something that Liz, who emphasized doing what you enjoy over money, found difficult to bear. They fell out over a trivial issue and didn't speak for years, until their mother was diagnosed with Alzheimer's.

It was not until their mother passed, that it was found she decided to write James out of her will, because he didn't need the money. James agreed, she didn't need the money. It was the timing of the change that irked him the most. His mother had changed her will shortly after moving in with Liz, at a time when her memory was poor, and she was not always of her right mind. Their late father had always insisted that they split the inheritance three ways, and until the move with Liz, their mother had always agreed.

Discussing the issue with Neil and Liz, Neil agreed that the estate should be split equally, whereas Liz wanted to uphold the will as it stood. When James decided to take the issue to court, it emerged that Liz had been spent $16,000 of their mother's money on her own dental work, a holiday for her family and musical tickets. She had justified to herself that as she was the main carer that she was entitled to dip into the funds early, and hadn't considered that the will would be contested.

The judge ruled in favour of James and Neil, seeing Liz as the "controlling force" behind the will change, and Liz was ordered to repay the $16,000. She still upholds that from her perspective she did nothing wrong, and some might agree. James feels there is no chance of resolving the feud now, and has resigned himself to not having any contact with his sister for the rest of his life. He feels that the dispute escalated far too quickly, and could have been avoided with a little more patience and understanding on both sides.

12

Conflict resolution

If you are experiencing difficulties and conflict within your family following the loss of a parent, it may help you to break down why this is happening, from your own perspective, the perspective of your relative, and that of an objective observer. Remember that no one can change the relationship you shared with a parent, and the memories an individual holds cannot be changed by any amount of arguing that can often arise within families at times like these.

Problems in families can get worse following a death. A once happy family may be thrown out of sync as everyone suddenly shows unexpected and often quite unusual behaviour. You might feel let down by a lack of support from people you thought you were close to, or the opposite- you may feel that all you need is to get away and you feel pressure from your family to go through things together or support someone else when you yourself feel weak.

Difficulties can arise from anywhere- from how to treat the dead person's possessions (some people may want to immediately get them out of the house and thrown away, whilst others may cling to them as though not touching them might somehow bring them back, or deny that anything has changed). Deciding how to go ahead with the funeral is such a sentimental, financial and practical matter that it can also be a source of conflict.

You can find a guided exercise that takes you through this process under "Family Conflict Resolution Exercise," in Section 3.

Section 3:

Grieving Exercises

13

At times of grief, look after yourself and give yourself time to recover. This is perfectly okay to do, and try not to be tempted to rush yourself or be too hard on yourself for not getting over any emotional ups and downs as quickly as you would like. If you want to take time off work, then consider that perhaps you should try to do so (with permission of course). If you feel like staying in and doing nothing, then consider allowing yourself to wallow for a while without being hard on yourself.

Grief can often be two steps forward, one step back. Add in all the twists and turns that your mind may take you through and it could be more of a long, sad dance, with no option to wait in the wings.

Although you can keep yourself busy, you might also beware of overworking yourself or burying yourself in activities that will allow you to hide from the pain. To recover you will need to go through it and experience it eventually. Saying that, if you feel you may be experiencing prolonged grief, then it may be time to seek ways of pulling yourself out of it. There are some guided exercises in the next section, that might help you process what you are feeling to move on.

Seek out or accept support that is given. Sharing your feelings and expressing what you're going through with others will help you to process your grief. It can be especially helpful to talk to others who have been through the same loss, as they will have had many similar feelings and will understand your experience. They may be able to shed some light on what to expect next, or give you the comforting feeling that you are not alone in your experiences.

It is best to avoid making life-altering decisions or drastic changes to your remaining relationships, as your clarity of thought is likely to be changed, and you may go on to regret the changes that you make when your frame of mind returns to normal later. One day you may think that everything is going well, the sun has come out and you have found your way back to how you used to be. The next you may feel completely lost and worse than ever. This really can lead to the feeling that you're making no progress at all. When you can't see how much further you must go, it makes you wonder how you will get through the bleakest moments, and if you're going to get there at all.

Having said that, I must tell you that arriving at your destination, where you make peace with your loss is not about "getting over it," but more about getting used to the idea that they are gone. The pain will still be there, but in a more manageable place, and you are more able to control your emotions when you visit the painful or happy memories of your loved one.

It is now eight years since my father died, and if I think about him, it can still feel like it was yesterday. The poignancy of loss creates a state of mind that will forever be easy to recall, and something that will never leave you. But personally, I am glad about that, because it is part of my on-going relationship with him.

Unfortunately, it is not possible to say how long the journey will last, because every person and every circumstance is different, but there are certain stages that most people pass through in the years following a significant loss. Arming yourself with knowledge about what these stages are can really help you to identify them in yourself, and help you realize that although what you are experiencing does not feel like progress, that you are recovering and have perhaps just passed to a new stage.

14

Guided Activities to Facilitate Healing

These guided exercises have been carefully chosen from professional counsellors, academics and mental healthcare professionals to help you process and progress through your loss as healthily as possible. This part of the book is interactive, so if you're using a tablet with a touchscreen, you can simply tap and hold on each exercise. On most devices a search icon will appear, and once you have removed your finger you'll be given a list of options. Selecting "note" or "notes" will let you add text, which can then be saved, so there's no need to use paper, unless you prefer it.

A Letter to Your Parent

Writing a goodbye letter is highly personal and can allow you to feel like you're talking directly to your lost loved-one about how you feel, how they have touched you and anything that's important.
.

I put a letter in my dad's coffin so that he would have it with him, and talked about all the lessons he had taught me in life, how I would miss him and how it felt now that he was gone. It might sound silly or spooky but occasionally I still write him an email, because with the internet being something you can't see or feel, it makes it feel as though there's still a direct connection there.

Everyone is different, and it's about finding a way that works well for you. You might keep the letter, put it in a memory box, mail it, leave it at a cemetery or burial ground, or pop it in a bottle and throw it into the sea or a lake. Speak from the heart, and directly to your parent, as though they are reading it.

Although this is a highly personal exercise, if you get stuck or don't know where to start, there are some ideas about what you might write about below.

I am saying goodbye because…
Saying goodbye makes me feel…
I remember when we…
You taught me…
Something I want you to know is…
I will always remember…

Exploring Memories

Another writing exercise involves exploring the memories of a lost parent. This can help not only keep their memory alive, but can help you start to process your emotions. However, this exercise can be very painful.

There are some ideas of the types of memories you might explore, if you need some help.

My earliest memory of you is…

My happiest memory of you is…
My funniest memory of you is…
Our best conversation was…
The most important thing you taught me is…
I'll never forget the day…
I'm grateful because…

What my Parent Would Want for Me

This third writing exercise is suitable for people who have been grieving for some time, and are having difficulty reconstructing their lives.

The objective of the exercise is to focus on what your parent would have wanted for you, and what they might say to you, if they could see how you were feeling, and what you were experiencing now.

Consider each of the following questions in turn:

If my parent could see how I was feeling, they would say…

Would my parent want me to feel this way?

How would they want me to feel?

If my parent could see how their death had affected my life, they would tell me...

Would my parent want my life to have been affected by their death in this way?

How would they want me to live my life?

My parent wanted me to do the following things during my life:

_____

_____

My parent wanted me to be the following things during my life:

_____

_____

My parent wanted me to have the following things during my life:

_____

_____

Creating a Remembrance Book or Box

Creating a remembrance book full of keepsakes can help you feel as though you are keeping your parent's story alive. This can be as simple as an envelope or as elaborate as a beautiful scrap book, photo album or memory box. Again- it's about what feels better for you.

Steps:
1. Firstly, decide if this is going to be a group or family activity, or a private activity.

2. Look at what memories and keepsakes you have. If you are sorting through a whole house of possessions, you are going to have a lot of choice about what to keep and what to throw or give away. Whereas if you have fewer items or some photographs you may find that you are faced with fewer decisions about what to include.

   My dad kept such a huge volume of sentimental memorabilia- that the house was full! Inevitably we had to give away, dispose of or sell the vast majority of his possessions and memories. Throwing so many sentimental items away felt heart wrenching to my brother, sister and me. As though we were doing something wrong or cold. Creating a memory box to keep some key moments from his life helped not only keep his memory alive for me, but helped to lessen the guilt and allowed me to let go of more of his belongings.

3. Decide how you want to keep your keepsakes and how you want to decorate or embellish them. Searching on Pinterest for "grief memory boxes" or "grief scrapbook" (as two examples), returns some really touching examples of how creative you can get with this if you wish. Some ideas include not only boxes and scrapbooks but jars, bottles or even little suitcases.

4. Shop for any supplies you need- like paint, glue or a pretty box, and get started. Think about labelling any old photographs, and

writing out any memories associated with each of your chosen keepsakes. Add poignancy by putting your memories together in a place that holds special significance to you and your parent, and you might even like to play music that brings up a special memory while you do so. If you wrote a letter to your parent already, you can include this into your keepsake place.

Charity Collection

If your parent died from an illness, or a particular cause was close to their heart, doing something for a charity that matches these causes and values, either alone or as a family or group, can be a beautiful way to honour them and give back to the world.

You can decide to get involved in charity work as much or as little as you like from a donation, to a collection, a bake sale, a sponsored jog, a marathon, or any number of challenges. Think about what suits your situation and if this is right for you and your family.

Thanking Care Staff

It is likely, unless your parent died unexpectedly, that healthcare professionals cared for your parent before their departure. Giving thanks to the hospital, ward or care staff that helped, in person or with a card, flowers, donation or small gift, can help give back to others, and subsequently help you with your own grief and difficult emotions.

Family Conflict Resolution Exercise

If you are the person in your family that is able to empathise well with others, and learn about emotions and other aspects of psychology (as I imagine you may be, because you are reading this book), then you may be able to start helping to heal the wounds in your family. Be aware, that you may not be thanked. Handle with care!

Look at the diagram which splits out conflict issues into various layers. The aim is to get a real understanding of the issue at hand, before you start to resolve it, so that you can talk your warring family, calmly and objectively through the exercise too.

How to understand and get to the heart of conflict

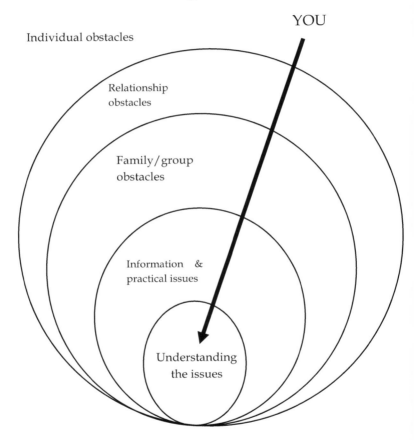

Layers of conflict resolution, adapted from Overcoming the Five Dysfunctions of a Family.

This exercise is for families who are experiencing conflict. Use your discretion to decide if this is an exercise best done by yourself in advance, or if you should bring the whole family together to attempt it at the same time.

To guide you through, I'm going to use an example of two people arguing over who should give a reading at your lost parent's funeral. Although this is a small example, it can give you an idea about how to think.

Your aunt thinks that she should perform a reading of your parent's favourite poem. Your *brother* would like to stand and deliver a speech about their favourite memories of your parent.

Personal Obstacles

The first stage is to think about the point of view of each person. In this case, your aunt feels that because she was always very close to your parent, that it should be her who gives a reading. Her main reason was a conversation she had when your parent asked for a particular poem as part of their funeral service, and your aunt sees this as part of their dying wishes.

Your brother feels as though he had a special relationship with your parent, who he sees as his closest family member. He feels as though he has been overlooked and silent within the family, but that your parent always stood up for him, believed in him and championed him when other people did not.

He thinks that the memorial speech should be delivered by himself, as one of the children, rather than your parent's sister.

The rest of the family, except for your grandparents, think that your brother should give the speech, and incorporate the poem into it as a compromise, but they don't want to get involved, in case they make the situation worse. Your grandparents are the only people being vocal, favouring your aunt delivering the speech, because she is the oldest sibling.

Think about your own family situation and write out the point of view of the first family member in the conflict.

Person 1's personal reasons for wanting what they want:

_____

Person 2's personal reasons for wanting what they want:

_____

Thirdly, how would an outside observer see the situation?

_____

Relationship Obstacles
Next is to think about the relationship between the two people that are arguing. Are past dynamics between the two opponents contributing to the struggle now?

_____

_____

Family Obstacles
Are there any family obstacles that are creating

issues? In our example, the grandparents favour their own eldest child making the speech, because it is the easiest, most obvious solution to them. They're not so interested in the emotional side of families, and are more interested in formalities.

This serves your aunt's wishes very well, as she feels backed up and in a strong position. Your brother, on the other hand, feels as though he is unable to speak up about his own wishes for fear of rocking the boat or being seen as selfish. He fears being verbally attacked or reprimanded if he brings the subject up again. His wife is pushing him to make his voice heard.

Objectively, we can see that both your aunt and brother have emotional needs that they want to express. It's not nice for your brother to feel too victimised or pressurised, and it's not very empathetic of your aunt to breeze over the feelings of your brother as though they don't matter.

What family dynamics are going on in your family? Are these related to underlying historical events or conflicts?

_____

_____

Objectively, which family dynamics are kind, considerate and positive?

_____

_____

Are there any family dynamics that could be considered the righting of past grievances?

_____

_____

Are there any family dynamics that are NOT empathetic, are spiteful, malevolent, control-oriented or cruel?

_____

_____

Practical Issues
Finally, are there any practical, financial or

pragmatic issues that are adding to this conflict? For example, sorting through possessions, executing the will, arranging or paying for the funeral, contacting insurance firms, selling assets... you get the idea.

Practical considerations affecting person 1:

_____

_____

Practical considerations affecting person 2:

_____

_____

Objective view of practical considerations:

_____

_____

Compromise
Now it's time to compromise and think through the options. What would person 1 and 2 consider to be fair compromises, and what would an objective

outsider consider to be fair?

In our case your aunt thinks that a good compromise would be if she were to read the poem in church, alongside your brother. Alternatively, she agrees that your brother might read his speech and say a prayer at the graveside during the burial.

Your brother also thinks that a good compromise would be a joint reading of the poem during the funeral service, with additional personal speeches made during the funeral service.

Consider some compromises for your family situation, trying to incorporate each person's emotional needs:

_____

_____

_____

_____

Be prepared to work through this exercise more than once before a place is reached that suits both parties.

Happiness Exercises

If you have been grieving for some time and are struggling to become happy again, you may think it is time that you became happier. The good news is that there are scientifically backed exercises you can do to improve how you feel overall. These are not related to grief specifically, and can be performed at any time, by anyone, to improve mood and outlook on life.

For anyone who is interested in learning more I would urge you to visit happify.com to read about this field and to take part in your own interactive, personalised exercise portfolio, that you can and even share with the online community there. Here I share a small amount of information on the science of happiness and one proven, highly effective exercise.

Scientists now know a considerable amount about what makes us happy. For an average person, happiness is approximately 50% down to our genes (they know this because of studies involving identical twins separated at birth), 40% because of recent major life events, both positive and negative.

These include things such as births, deaths, promotions, marriages, divorces, and even buying your dream house. This proportion of your happiness during grief will be greatly diminished, and will increase back to baseline levels over time. Any happy events will also create a temporary increase in this proportion of your overall happiness.

Grief is a major life event, and in my case, it took me at least two years before I could accept what had happened. This may seem a long time, but if you look at the overall picture, for the vast majority of people it does not last forever, even though it may seem as though it will. For almost everyone, the sun will come up, the birds will sing, and most people will become positive again.

For many life events, the science of happiness shows that our ability to judge how life events will affect our happiness is poor. For example, if we compare two groups of people, one of which has unexpectedly won millions in a lottery, whilst the other has suffered a catastrophic spine injury, you might expect that the lottery winners would have an elevated happiness-level six months after the win, and paraplegics would be substantially less happy.

You would be wrong. It is the other way around, people who became paraplegic are almost as happy as they were before their accident, and the lottery winners are not anywhere near as happy. Unexpected isn't it?

Lottery winners find themselves elated, stunned and with a world of possibilities before them. After some time, with an abundance of wealth to utilise, they realise that they are now out of context with their friends, families and communities, perhaps even feeling as though they can no longer relate to the, or that money has come between them.

They have to readjust their aspirations, perhaps even writing off what they considered to be "good work," having worked towards life or economic goals for many years, which can feel as though it was a waste of time. They need new goals.

After six months they are still working through the psychological adjustment period. Paraplegics on the other hand are plunged into shock at what they have lost straight away at the time of the event. Six months further on, they have made more headway in terms of adjusting their aspirations, and are generally receiving a great deal of support from family, friends and their community.

For most people approximately 10% of their happiness is down to controllable elements, that don't include major life events. Scientists have done a great deal of research determining what factors affect a person's sense of happiness, and this controllable portion can be influenced by surprisingly specific things, both practicable skills and elements within our lives.

Five key skills that increase happiness levels are: savouring experiences, practising gratitude, aspiring towards a goal, giving generously or helping others, and empathizing with others. Each of these skills has a guided exercise below.

In terms of life elements, certain parts of our lives have also been shown to increase our sense of wellbeing: family and friends, community, work and having faith in something larger than yourself. Incorporating the key skills of happiness into these various aspects of our lives is a no brainer.

Giving, helping and empathizing skills can be applied to family and friends, work and the community in which you live to help your loved ones, colleagues and those in need. In turn this makes your life more positive. Aspiring towards a goal can also be applied to your work life, as well as your personal goals related to faith.

A faith does not need to be religious, but simply gives some context; allowing you to see how you fit into the vast universe and planet, whilst maintaining an optimistic outlook. My faith is not religious; but do I have faith in human nature, love and I firmly believe most people get joy from doing good. It has been shown that people who have a belief system (such as religious faith, spirituality, or faith in basic human nature), have been shown to be happier than those who do not.

Happiness from work comes from feeling as though you are contributing something of value for yourself and for others. It also comes from feeling as though your life and work are your "own enterprise" or under your own control to build up as you would like- another reason why grief gives us such a knock- it removes our sense of being to control our own destiny and reminds us of how vulnerable we are.

If you find yourself struggling to be happy working on these elements may help you get back on track as you come to the end of your grieving process. Studies have shown that being frequently grateful has a significant effect on our happiness and wellbeing, as does listing your three favourite things of the day.

One immediate task you can do now to make yourself start feeling better is set a reminder every day, perhaps at the end of your work day, before you go to bed, or at dinner time if you wish to share with your family- telling you to list your 3 favourite things of the day and 1 thing each day that you are grateful for in your life.

Studies have shown that doing this every day for 2 weeks has beneficial effects on your sense of wellbeing more than 6 months later, and is better for your happiness than going on vacation.

Journaling in general has a similar beneficial effect, but this particular task encourages optimism, whereas journaling allows you to explore your emotions. This is not always helpful if you are suffering from complicated grief and are rehashing your feelings rather than processing them and moving forwards.

You may find doing this as a family has a wonderful effect on everybody. Whenever you're feeling low you can reread your list. I find that my list is almost entirely made up of what I've eaten that day! I never realised I was so food oriented before!

3 Favourite things of the day:

1._____

2._____

3._____

1 thing I am grateful for:

_____

Grief Support Groups and Counselling Services

If you are feeling as though you are unable to cope, are not moving on as you should be, or if you simply want to talk to someone about how you feel, grief support groups and counselling can be great way to ensure that the grief is worked through healthily and to help prevent prolonged or perpetual grief. There are some listed below:

- **soulcareproject.org/**
1. US based service with information on grief, as well as chats with a counsellor by phone, email or even video call.

- **https://www.griefshare.org/**
2. Thousands of meeting groups around the world, but mainly in the US and Canada, that meet weekly. You can search directly for your nearest group using your town or postcode.

- **http://www.onlinegriefsupport.com/**
3. An online community where people share their bereavement feelings and experiences.

- **http://www.cruse.org.uk/**
4. UK based bereavement care service, with in person meeting groups and telephone helpline.

You can find many more services by simply searching Google for "grief support." Many of the search results that are returned will be local to your area, because Google searches the internet based on your location. So, if you don't find what you are looking for at the links above, please do try this.

15

Final Word

Grieving comes in many shapes and forms, and has no definite length of time. The sadness that accompanies bereavement can often look similar to depression. However, this sorrow is usually a normal response to losing someone important. When a parent dies it may even feel as though part of your identity has died- a person who built you, into you.

Death may bring life to an end, but it does not end a relationship. Eventually, you will readjust to a new relationship in which you may still feel your parent's presence.

The relationships within your family may or may not feel strained for a while, but these are the relationships you will continue into life with, and where possible should be nurtured with forgiveness and compassion.

Whilst it is not possible to understand your exact circumstances, or even begin to predict the complicated web of memories and feelings that losing a parent stirs up in you, please don't think that what you are going through is going to last forever.

If you think that you are experiencing prolonged or complicated grief or depression, then be kind to yourself and look after yourself. If you really want to feel better, you may find some further reading on the Science of Happiness and performing some daily Happiness rituals is a good starting point from here.

Look to your friends, family and professional support and medical services to get help and find out what it is that you need to move forwards. Perform practical exercises, and force yourself to tend to your own needs. Try and find your way back to a path of hope, with new aspirations and goals. It's okay if you need help doing this.

LOSS OF A PARENT

Most people reach a point in time when they look to the future with optimism. It took me a long time to reach this point, but having reached it I can honestly say that I can think of my dad and only smile. I hope that you find this place too, and carry positive memories of your parent with you into a bright new future.

Bibliography

1. Research on Bereavement after Caregiving, accessed on PubMed 2016:

    https://www.ncbi.nlm.nih.gov/pmc/articl es/PMC2790185/

2. Impact of Grief on the Family System, accessed on Wiley 2016:

    http://onlinelibrary.wiley.com/doi/10.104 6/j..1983.00623.x/pdf

3. The Science of Happiness, accessed on happify.com 2016:

    http://www.happify.com/public/science-of-happiness/

4. Conflict Resolution: Changing Perspectives, accessed on Psychology Today 2016:

    https://www.psychologytoday.com/blog/ turning-point/201506/3-steps-resolving-conflict-within-your-family

List of Figures

The seven stages of grief (modified from Kubler-Ross five stages of grief)

Parenting styles

How to understand and get to the heart of conflict

ABOUT THE AUTHOR

Okay, okay, the secret's out… Amazon bestselling author, 'Theresa Jackson,' is a pen name. The alternative identity of a popular non-fiction writer. She's relishing in the freedom to explore sensitive issues like family, sex, grief and relationships, without the risk of alienating her nearest and dearest.

Don't you just wish you could say what you really think? Join 'Theresa,' and let it out. Jump on the exploration freight train and get a greater understanding of yourself and others.

BOOKS BY THERESA JACKSON

How to Handle a Narcissist (Excerpt follows)

The Science of Strong: Build Success through Emotional Resilience

Loss of a Parent, Adult Grief when Parents Die

Excerpt from:

HOW TO HANDLE A NARCISISST

Understanding and Dealing with a Range of Narcissistic Personalities

Researching this book has revealed how much misinformation abounds about narcissism, amongst informed, expert research. The subject is a hotbed of mismatching and oversimplified ideas; with a conflicting sense of what "healthy" self-enhancement is and what is "not."

*Much of the misguided rhetoric published online takes a black and white approach, as though narcissism is a pure and straight forward "label" rather than a range of healthy and unhealthy reactions and behaviors, triggered in **98% of people** (including you, it is highly likely). These behaviors are present in varying intensities, for varying amounts of the time. Reactions depend not only on seemingly permanent, underlying thought- processes, but on what's going on in life, right now (and recently), that might be aggravating usually dormant self-esteem issues.*

Narcissism exists on a spectrum from low levels to high. Some narcissism is healthy, and is part of our normal responses to having our ego threatened, allowing us to

EXCERPT FROM "HOW TO HANDLE A NARCISSIST"

maintain our sense of self without suffering from crushing shame and a sense of defeat. At the top of the scale is the personality disorder known as narcissistic personality disorder (NPD) characterized by a haughty sense of superiority, an inflated sense of importance and a deep need for admiration.

This book takes a more nuanced approach to the narcissistic scale. We won't simply be talking about how to deal with those that are diagnosable with NPD, but also about the majority of narcissistic people who fit lower down, and are relatable to most people. We'll attempt to decipher how narcissistic the person you are dealing with is, give you a better understanding of their thoughts, feelings and motivations, and help you determine whether you should cut them out of your life, or "manage" them to a greater or lesser extent.

In some cases, you might find it would be better for your wellbeing to continue a more limited relationship with them. Whether to cut off from a narcissistic mother, for example, is a hugely important decision that affects you for the rest of your life, whereas cutting off from a friend will have less of an impact on your life in the long term. You may have a narcissistic partner that is not diagnosable with NPD (for example, not overwhelmed with narcissistic responses, most of the time, nor fitting most of the diagnostic criteria), but does display frequent damaging

EXCERPT FROM "HOW TO HANDLE A NARCISSIST"

narcissistic behaviors that have severely impacted your "sense of safety" and trust in your relationship.

Here I will share examples of those who have found contentment by managing and restructuring the paradigm of their relationships with narcissistic people who are non-abusive. We have case studies from other people who have found themselves contemplating the decision of whether to cut off from their narcissistic family members, partners and friends, and what the outcome was for them.

Feeling angry, humiliated or as though you want to help or change narcissistic people is only natural. This can be incredibly tough to come to terms with. This book focuses only on what you can do for yourself, including managing the boundaries of your relationship, and asserting yourself as an independent person in your own right. If you are interested in helping, changing, or even if you are feeling vengeful towards a narcissist, I urge you to proceed with caution.

COMING SOON...

"Next up, I'll be diving into how to build emotional resilience and follow your dreams. A step by step guide to jumping off the metaphorical cliff, and setting your sights on happiness.

On the dangerous side, I'm excited to be dipping into the world of dark psychology. I'll be writing a guide on how to manage people in your life who seem to have little to no conscience, and sit high on the psychopathic scale. I'll include a section for women on how to avoid dating men with psychopathic, narcissistic, Machiavellian or sadistic personality traits, that continue to trawl the dating scene. Some of the advice will come straight from the mouths of psychopaths and manipulative characters themselves, so it should make for an interesting read!

Sticking with the theme of dangerous love, after I've toyed with the psychos and sadists, I'll be going after the womanizers too, to see what advice they can offer to ladies looking for love. After a chance meeting with a 'player-trainer' in Cologne a couple of years ago, the subject of 'the game' (or womanizing as it used to be called) has fascinated me ever since. The player I ran into was hosting a seminar to teach men how to bed women, and had published a book 'How to f* on the first date.' Charming. Let's see what happens when I attend one of their training seminars and speak to them first hand.

The next book in my narcissism series will be investigating if narcissists can be helped, and if so, why so many of them never change. Could you help a narcissist if you wanted to? What potential new therapies are there in development?

If you would like to know when the next book is ready or to be kept informed of special offers, freebies and giveaways, email me at theresa.jackson.books@gmail.com and I'll add you to my readers list. Be sure to tell me which subject you like the sound of, best!

Theresa."

FOLLOW MY WORK

If you would like to receive news of book releases, giveaways and special offers you can follow my work on Goodreads, Amazon and Facebook, or email me at theresa.jackson.books@gmail.com and I'll add you to my readers list.

Thanks for your support!
Theresa.

Leave a review...

If you enjoyed this book, found it useful or otherwise then I'd really appreciate it if you would post a short review on Goodreads, Amazon or wherever you purchased the book. I do read all the reviews personally so that I can continually write what people are wanting.

Made in the
USA
Monee, IL